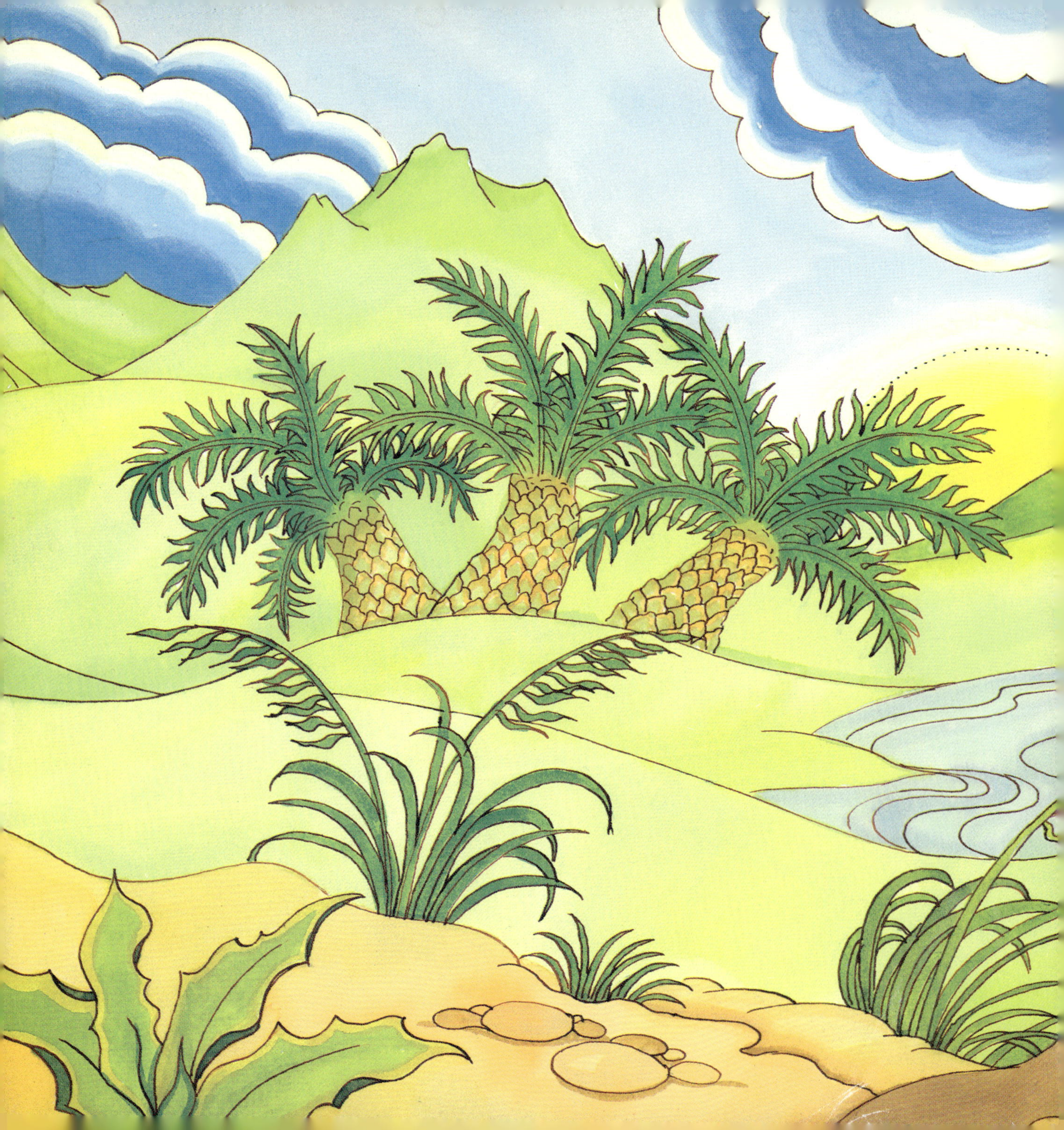

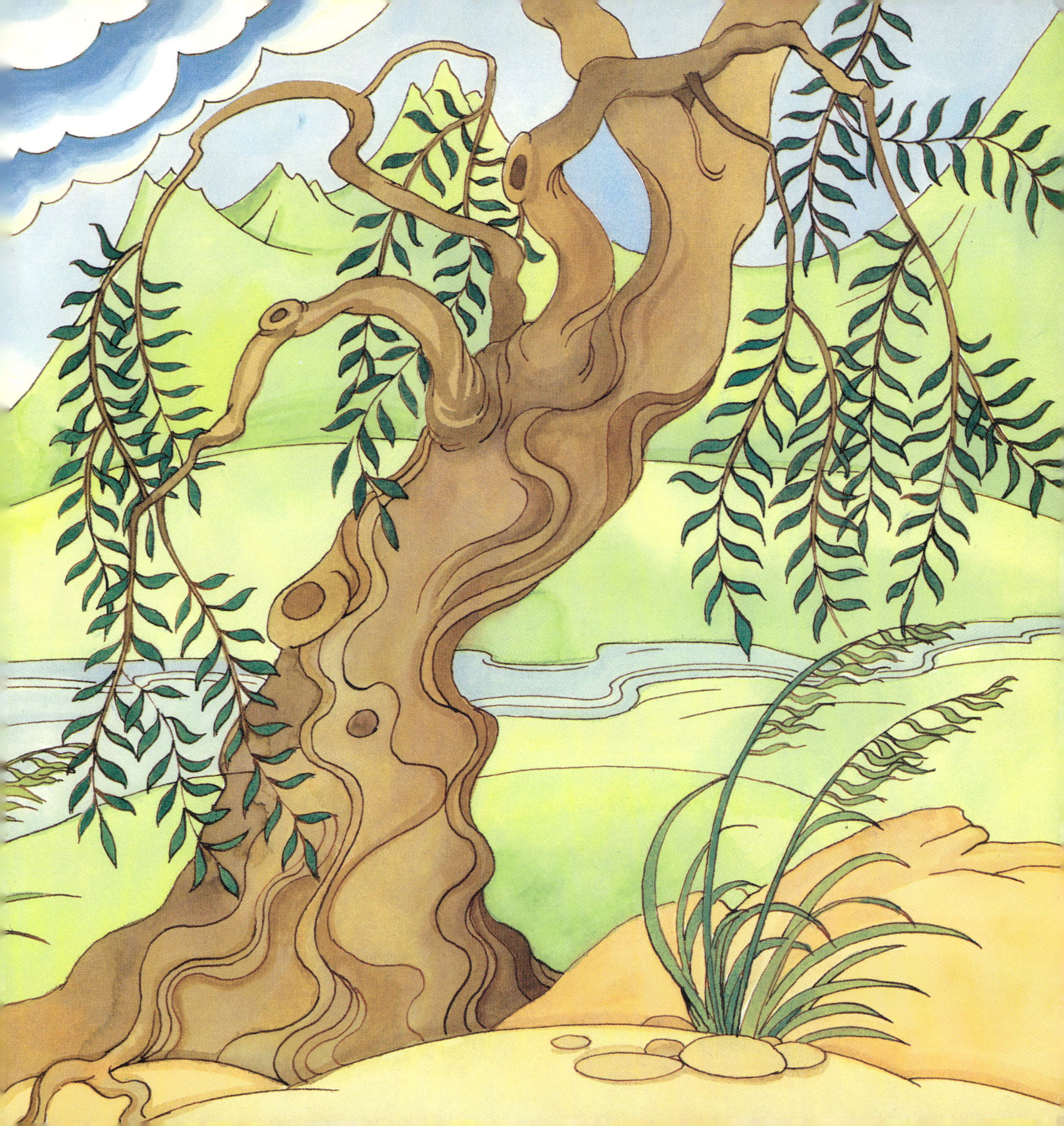

Flying Frog Publishing, Inc.
Auburn, Maine 04210 U.S.A.
Copyright © 1996 Flying Frog Publishing, Inc.
Flying Frog Publishing and the associated pictorial device are registered trademarks of Flying Frog Publishing, Inc.
All rights reserved. No part of this publication may be reproduced, stored in a retrieval system, or transmitted in any form or by any means, electronic, mechanical, photocopying, recording or otherwise, without the prior consent of the copyright owner.
Printed in Canada

DANIEL IN THE LIONS' DEN

Retold by Ronne Randall
Illustrated by Sara Sliwinska

Flying Frog Publishing

A long time ago, a boy called Daniel lived in Jerusalem. When Nebuchadnezzar, the king of Persia, invaded Jerusalem, he took Daniel into his household to be educated and brought up like one of his own children.

Daniel had a good life in the royal household. But he never forgot his God. He prayed to God every day, and in everything he did, he followed the word of God.

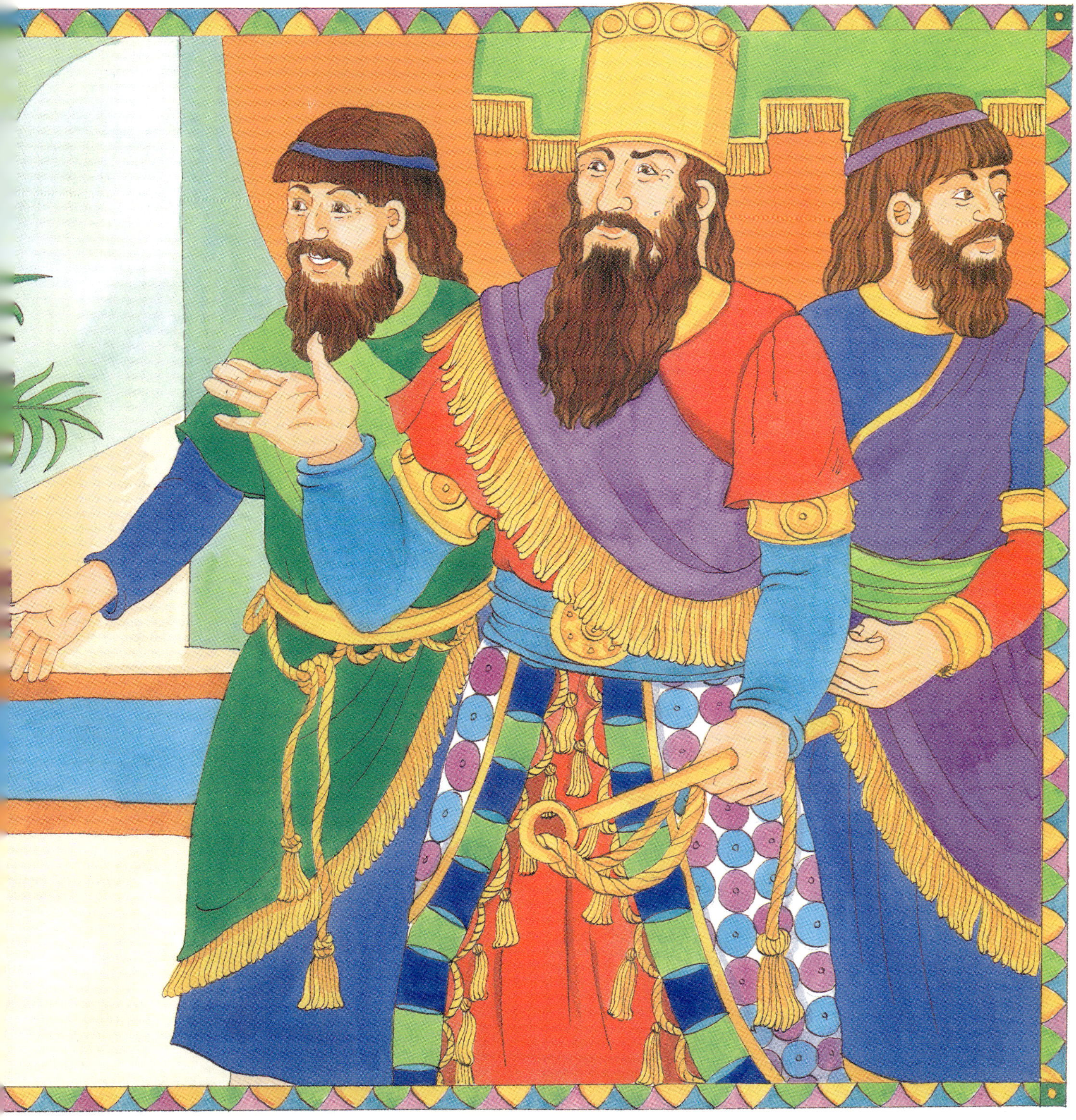

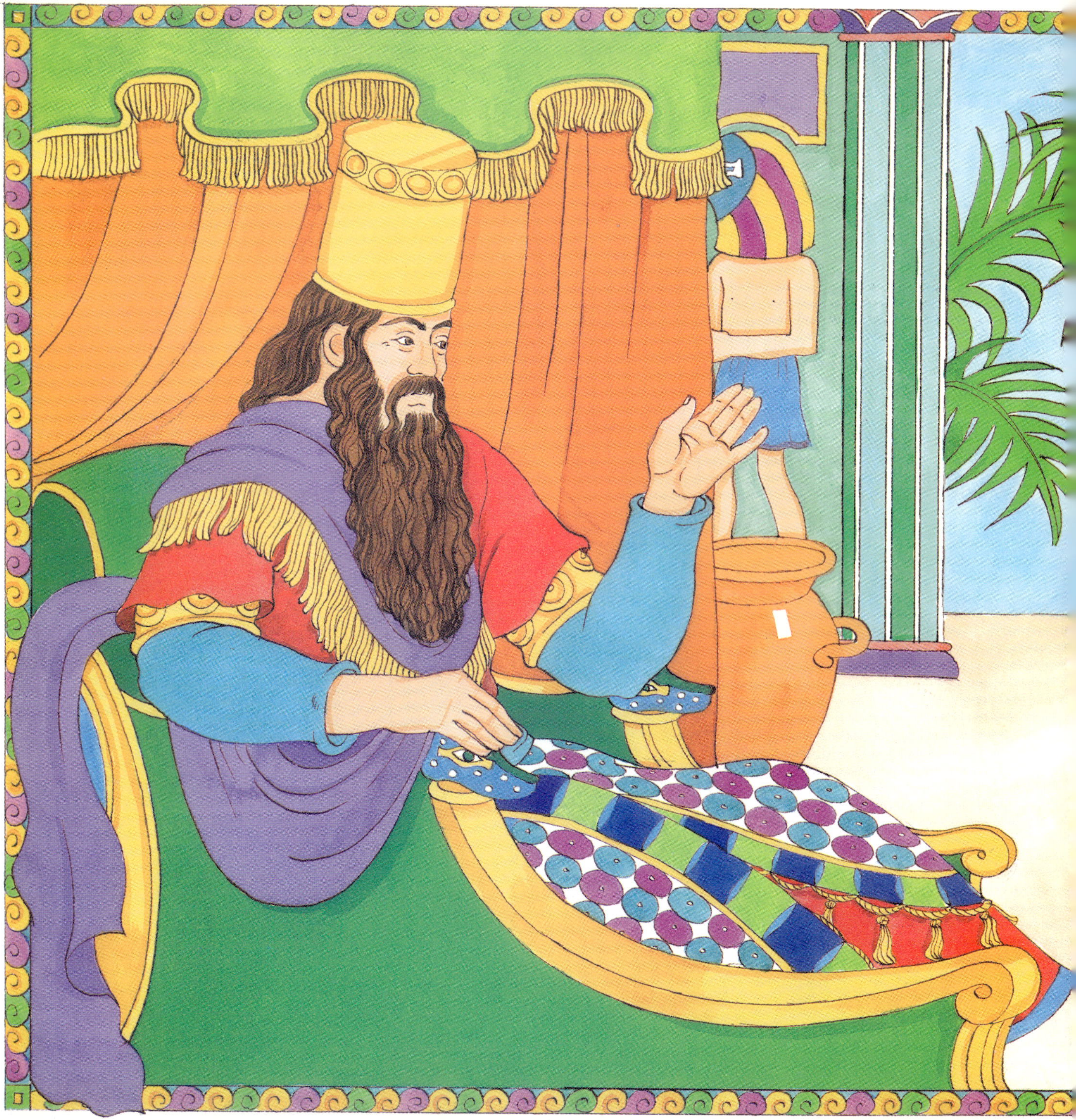

Daniel grew to be a young man of great wisdom. When the king had bad dreams, Daniel prayed to God for understanding. Then he was able to explain the king's dreams to him so that he could sleep peacefully.

King Nebuchadnezzar so loved and trusted Daniel that he made him his chief adviser.

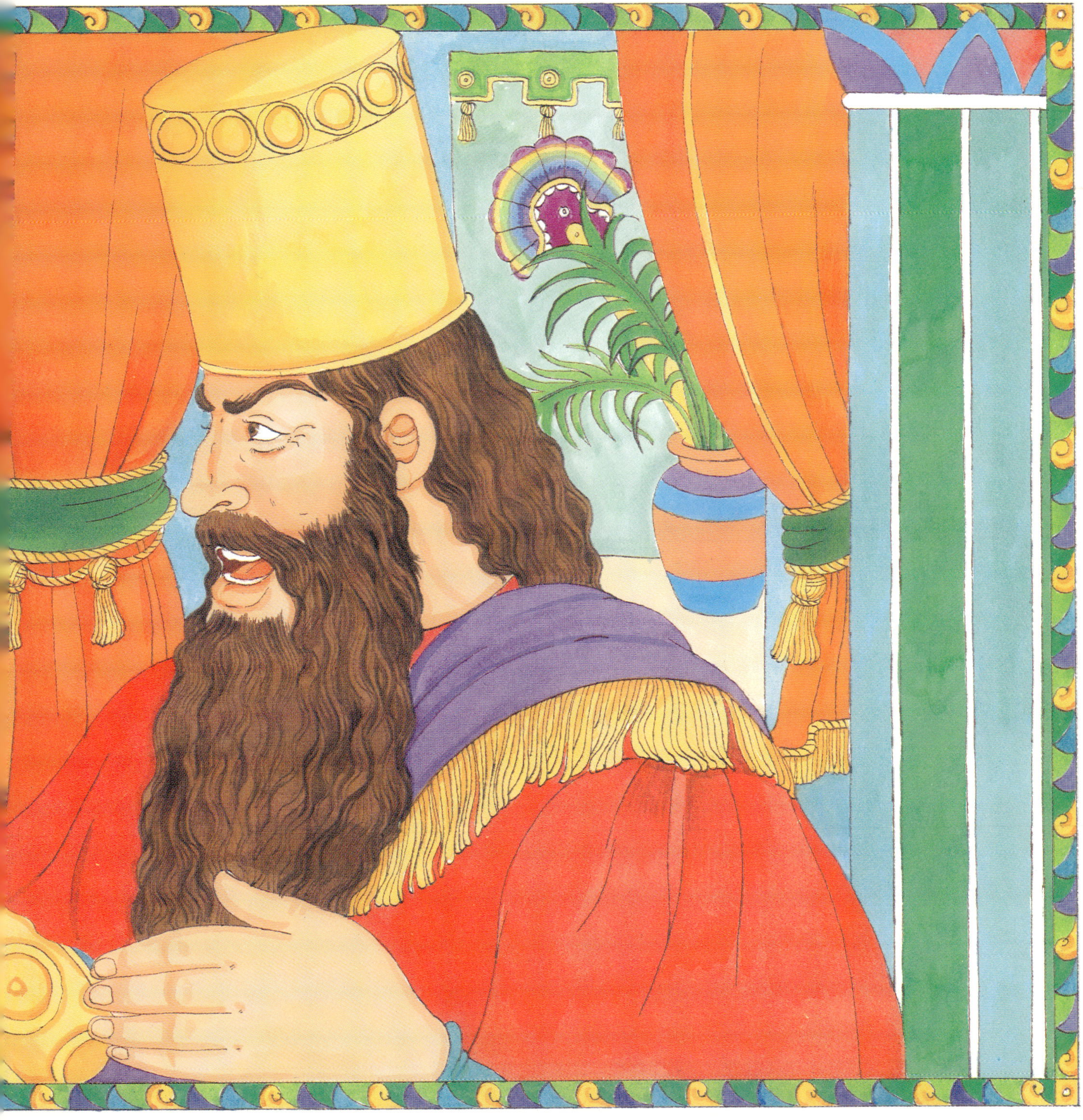

When a new king, Darius, came to the throne, he appointed 120 officials and three presidents to govern the land. And he made Daniel the highest president of all.

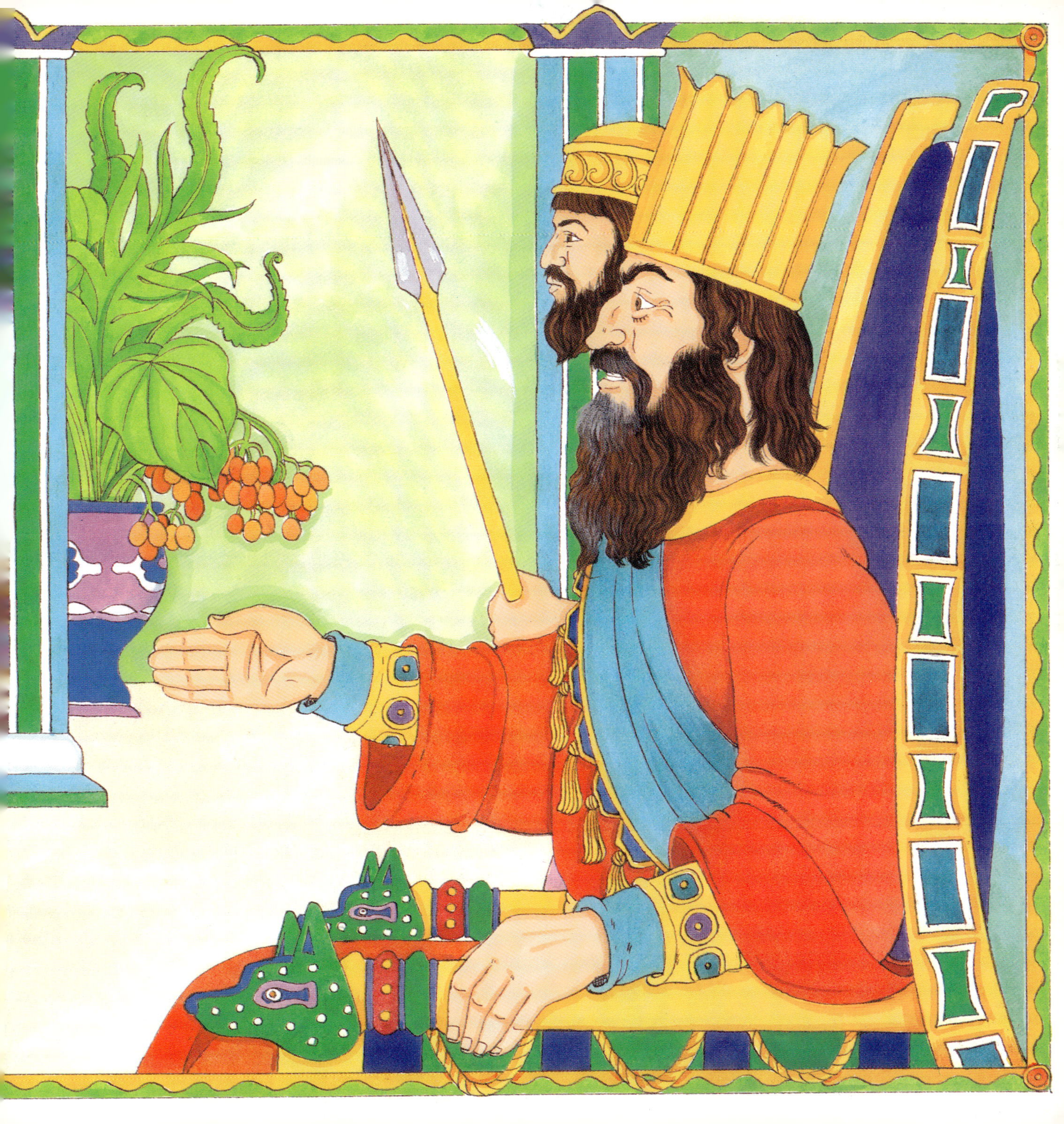

Because King Darius admired Daniel above everyone, the other officials were jealous of him. They decided to find a way to make King Darius get rid of him.

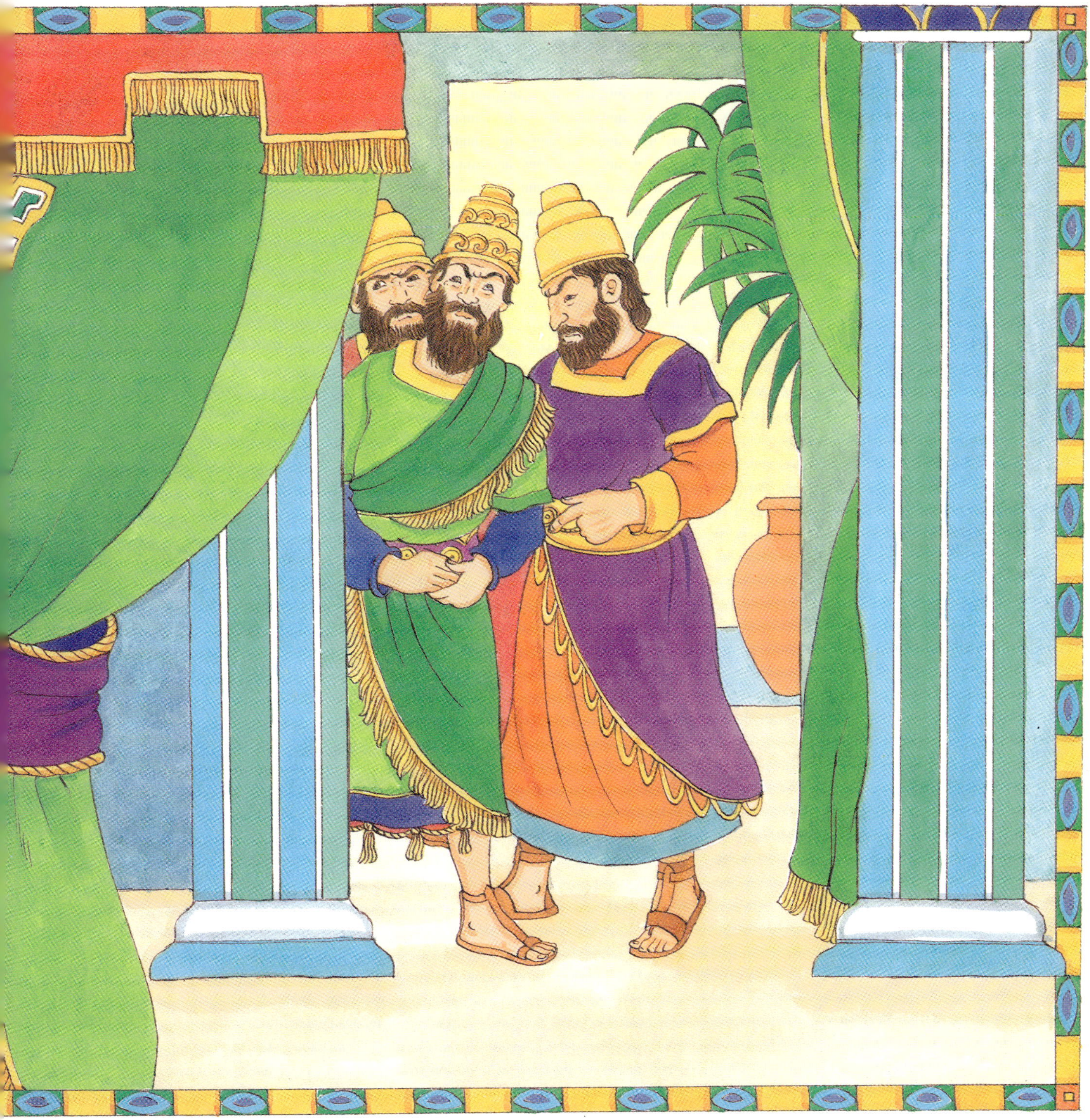

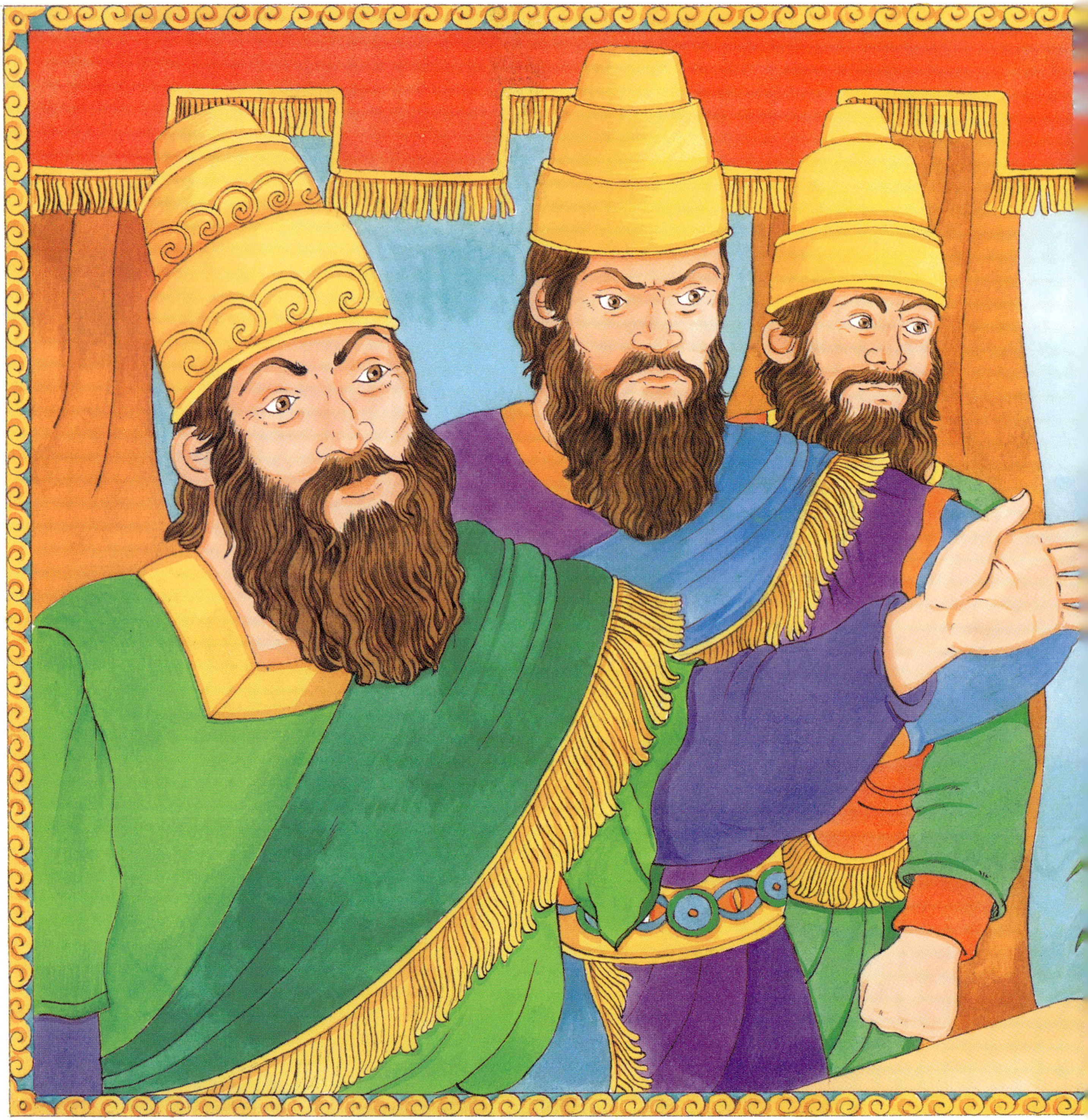

The officials knew that Daniel worshiped God and obeyed God's laws. So they said to King Darius, "O great and mighty King, we think so highly of you that we think you should make a new law: everyone in your kingdom should worship only you, and bow down only to you. Anyone who is found praying to anyone but you should be thrown into a den of hungry lions!"

King Darius was flattered by these words, and he signed the law.

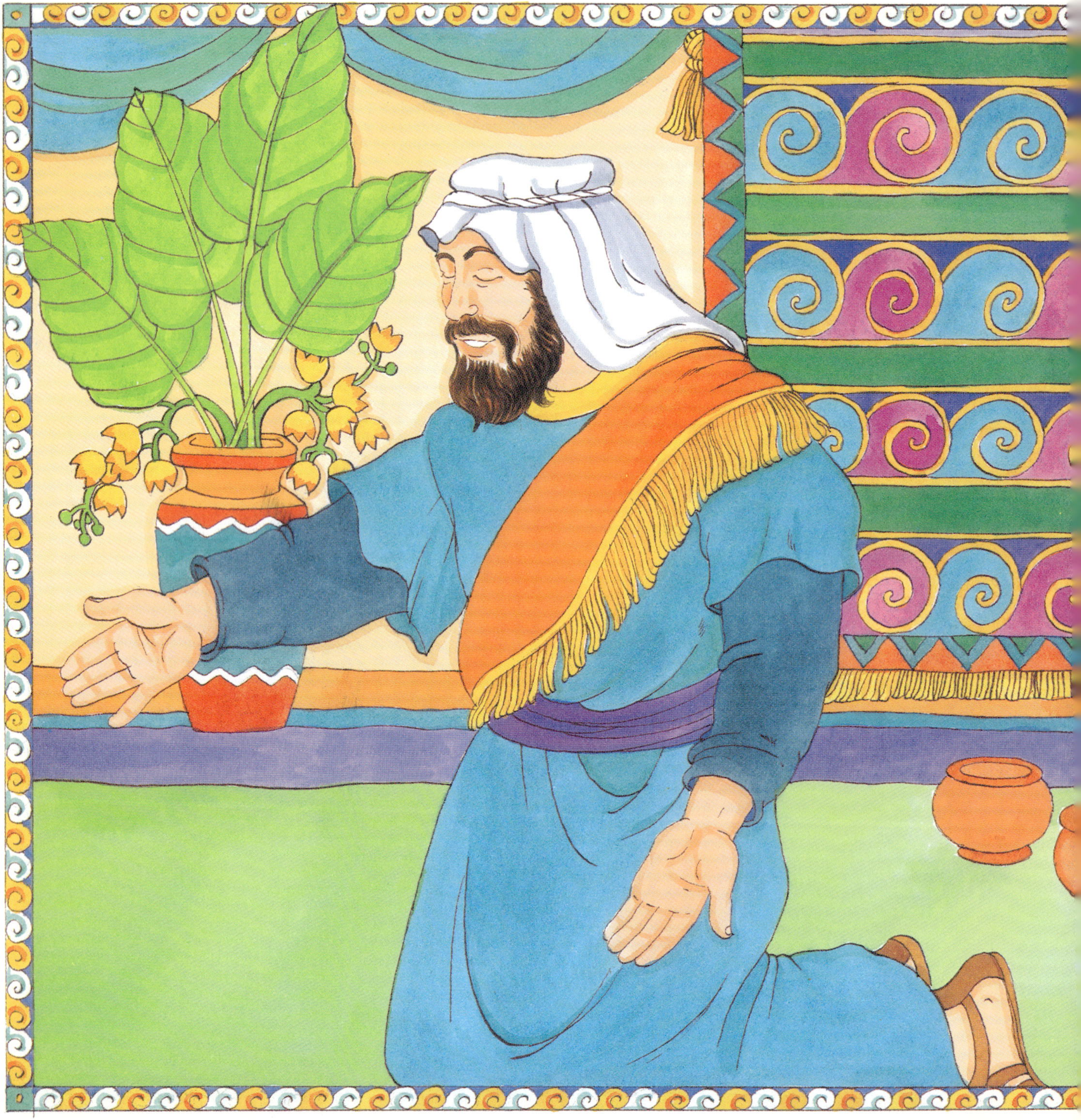

When Daniel heard about the new law, he went to his home and did what he did every day: he knelt down and prayed to God.

The officials were spying on Daniel, and as soon as they saw him praying, they rushed to tell the king.

"O great and mighty King," they said, "Daniel has broken your new law! We saw him kneeling down and praying to his God. If he thinks his God is more important than you are, he must be punished. Throw him into a den of lions!"

When the king heard this, he was very upset, for he did not want Daniel to be hurt. He realized that his officials had tricked him. He tried to think of a way to rescue Daniel, but there was nothing he could do. The law had to be obeyed.

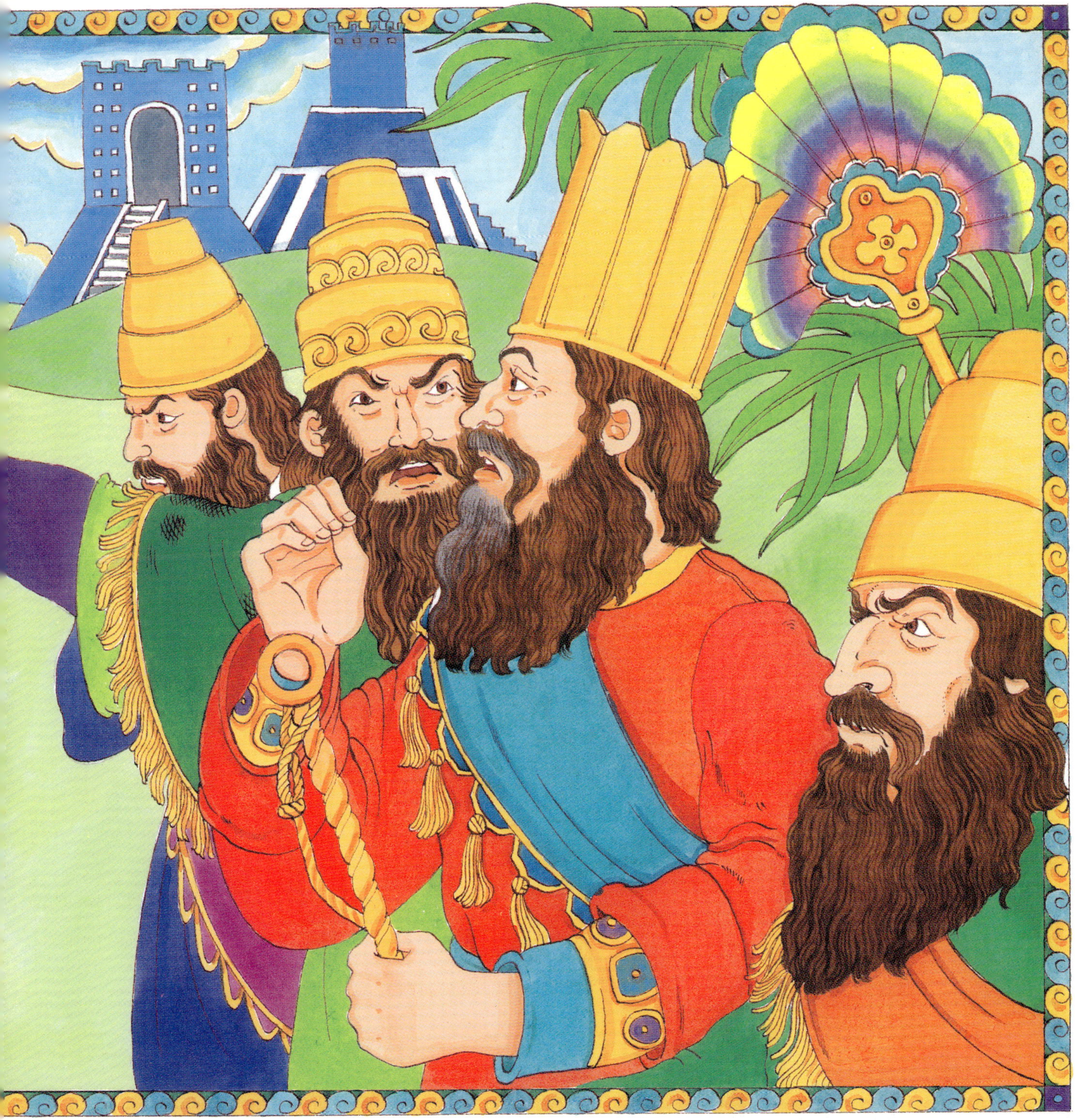

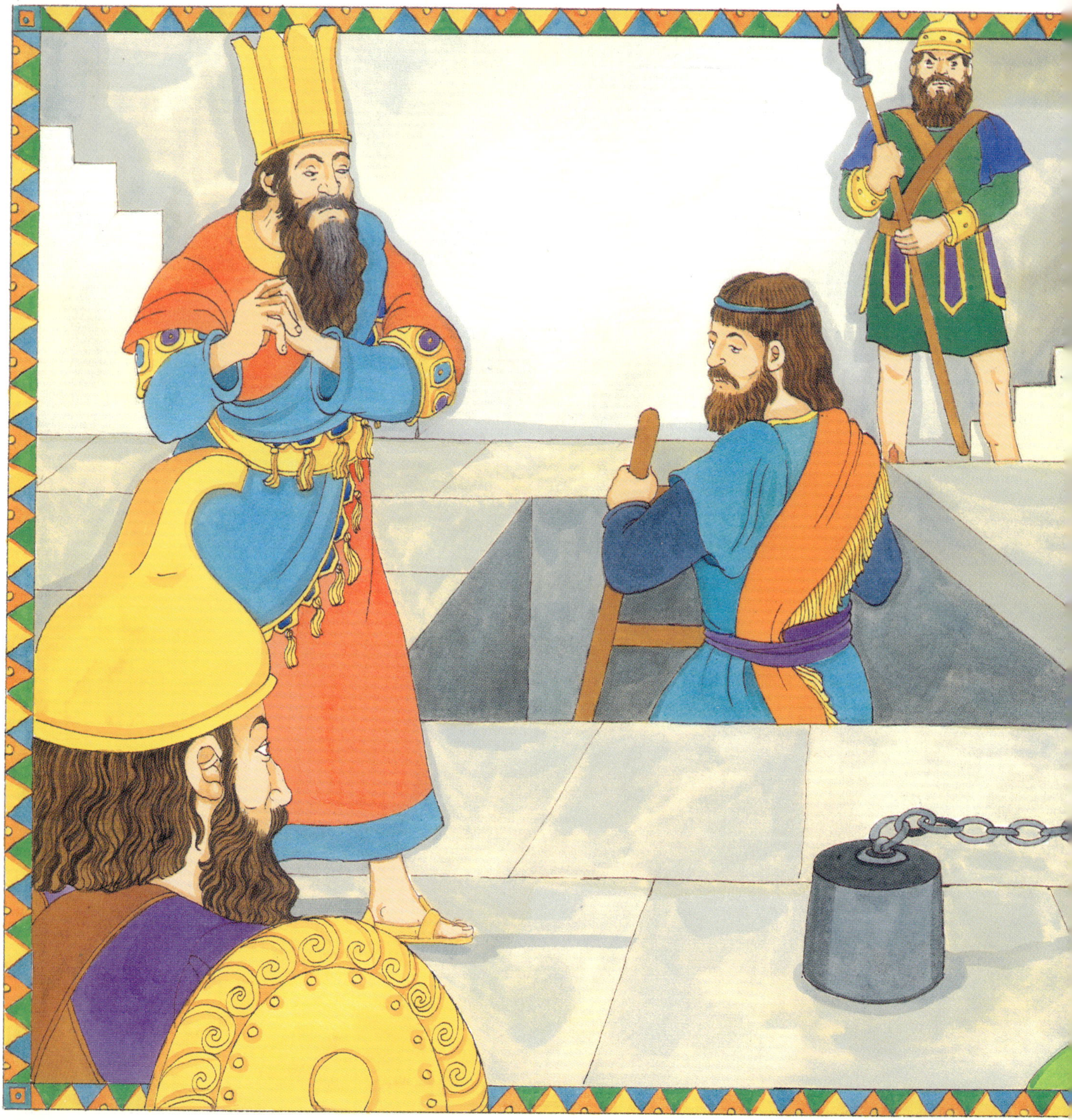

"Pray to your God," King Darius said to Daniel. "I hope he can save you!"

Daniel was put into a den of fierce lions. To make sure that Daniel could not escape, a stone was put over the mouth of the den, and the king sealed it shut with his own seal.

The king went back to his palace with a sad and troubled heart. He was so unhappy that he would not eat and could not sleep. He stayed awake all night, worrying about Daniel.

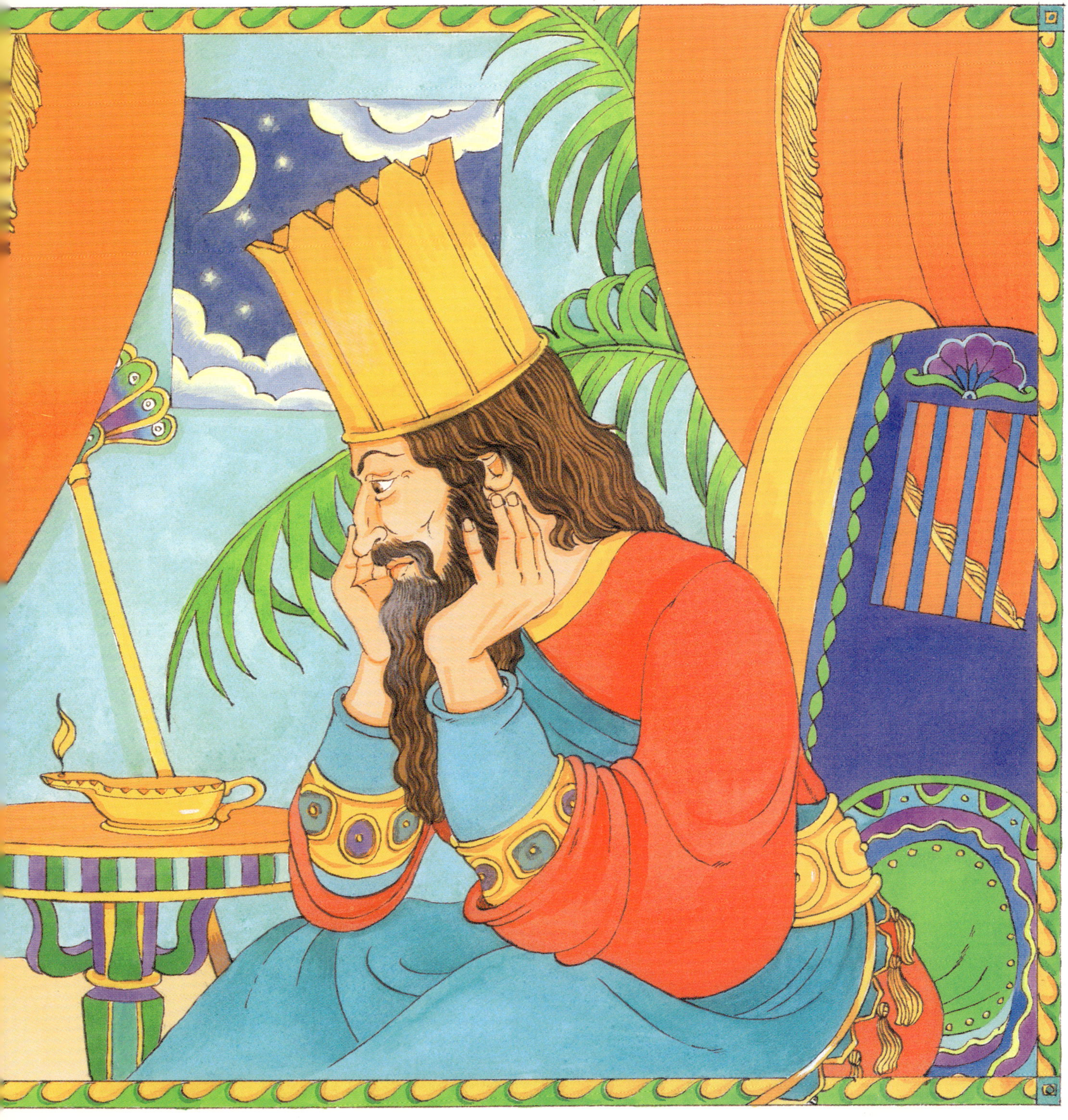

In the morning, the king rushed to the lions' den and called out, "Daniel! Daniel! Has your God saved you?"

To the king's joy and amazement, Daniel replied, "Yes! He sent an angel to protect me, and the lions have not harmed me at all."

The happy king set Daniel free, and ordered that the men who had tricked him should be thrown to the lions instead.

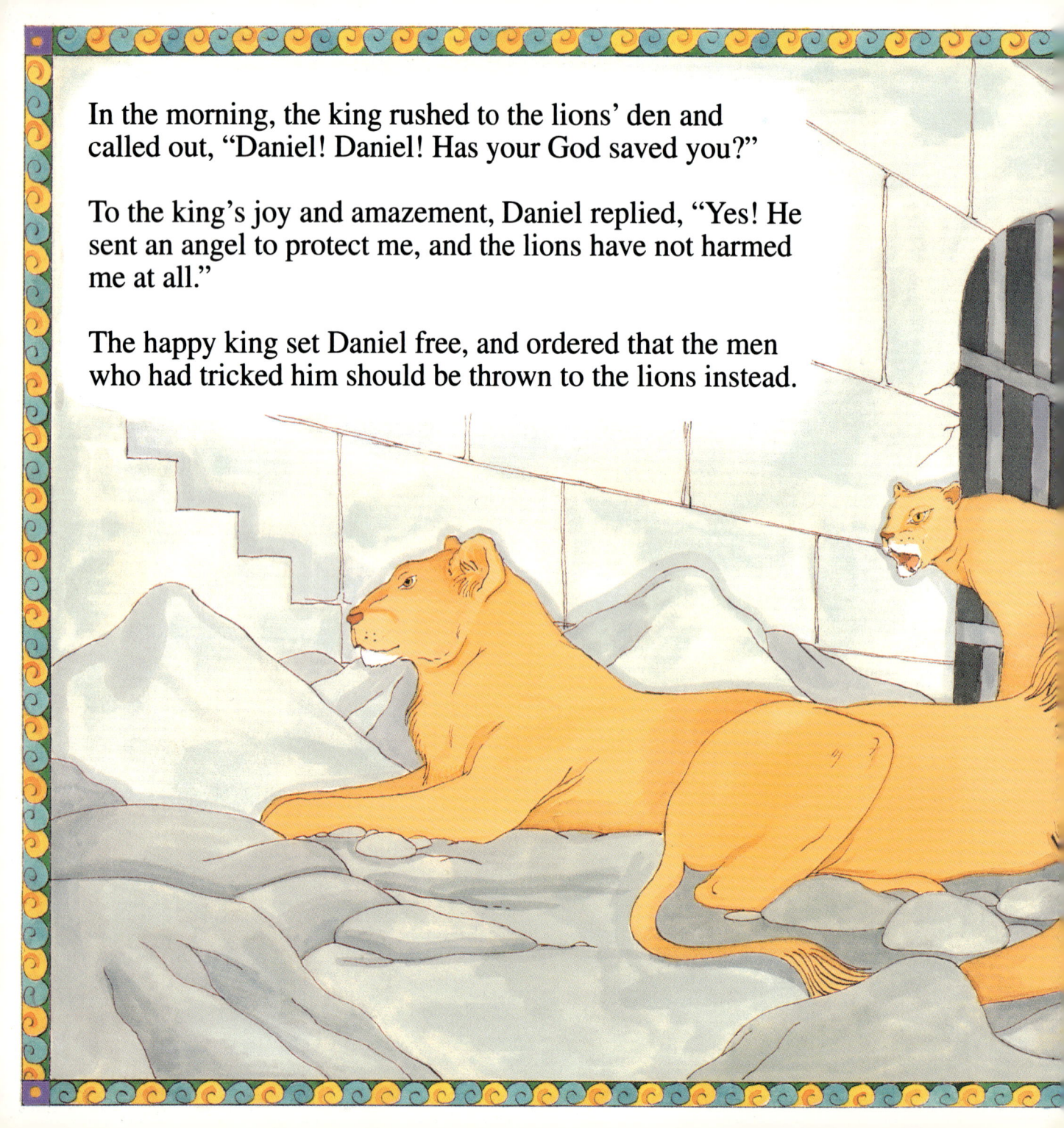

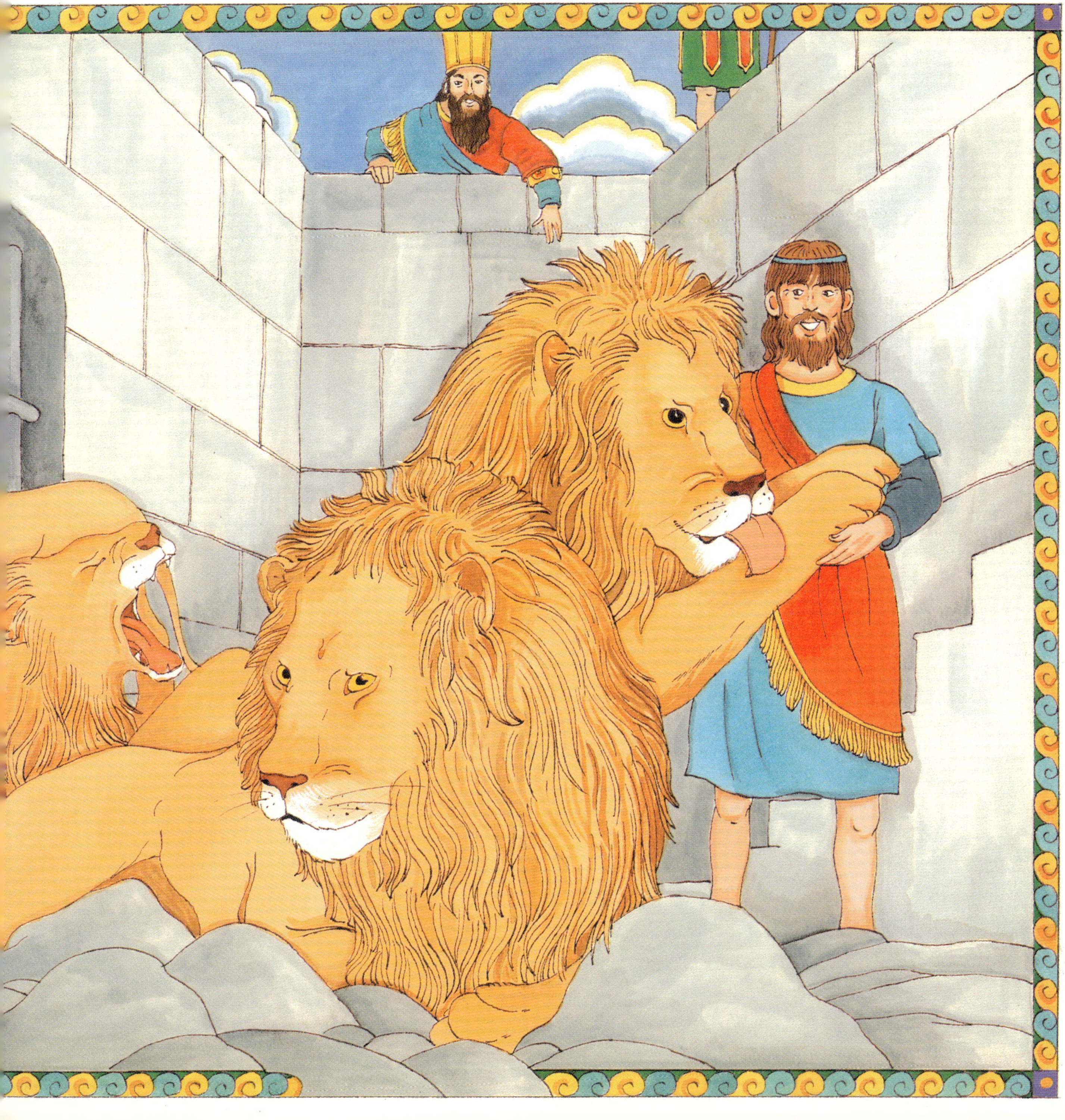

Then King Darius declared before all his people that Daniel's God was the one true God of heaven and earth. And for the rest of King Darius' reign, Daniel lived happily. He was free to worship God, and he was loved and respected by all.

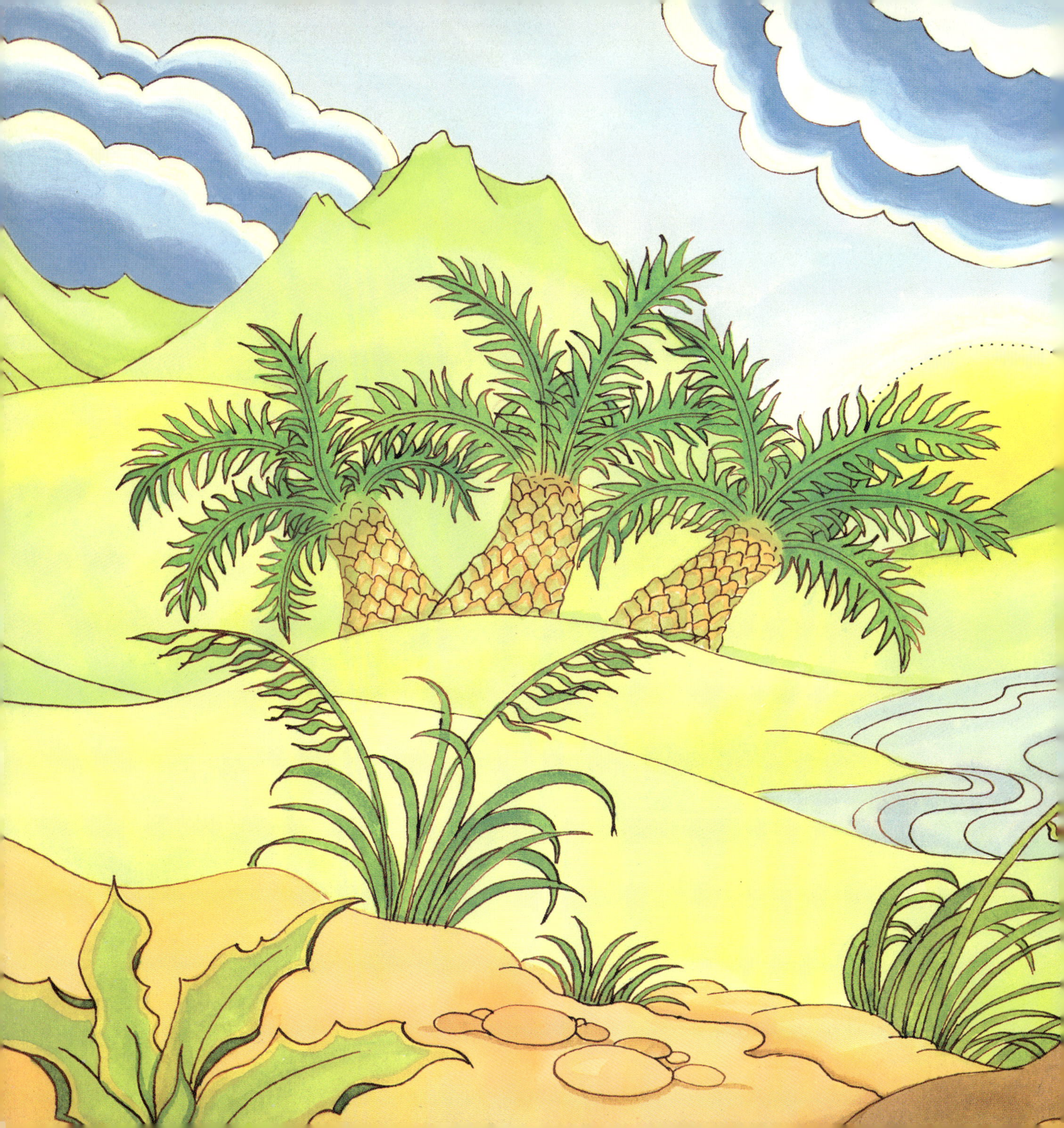

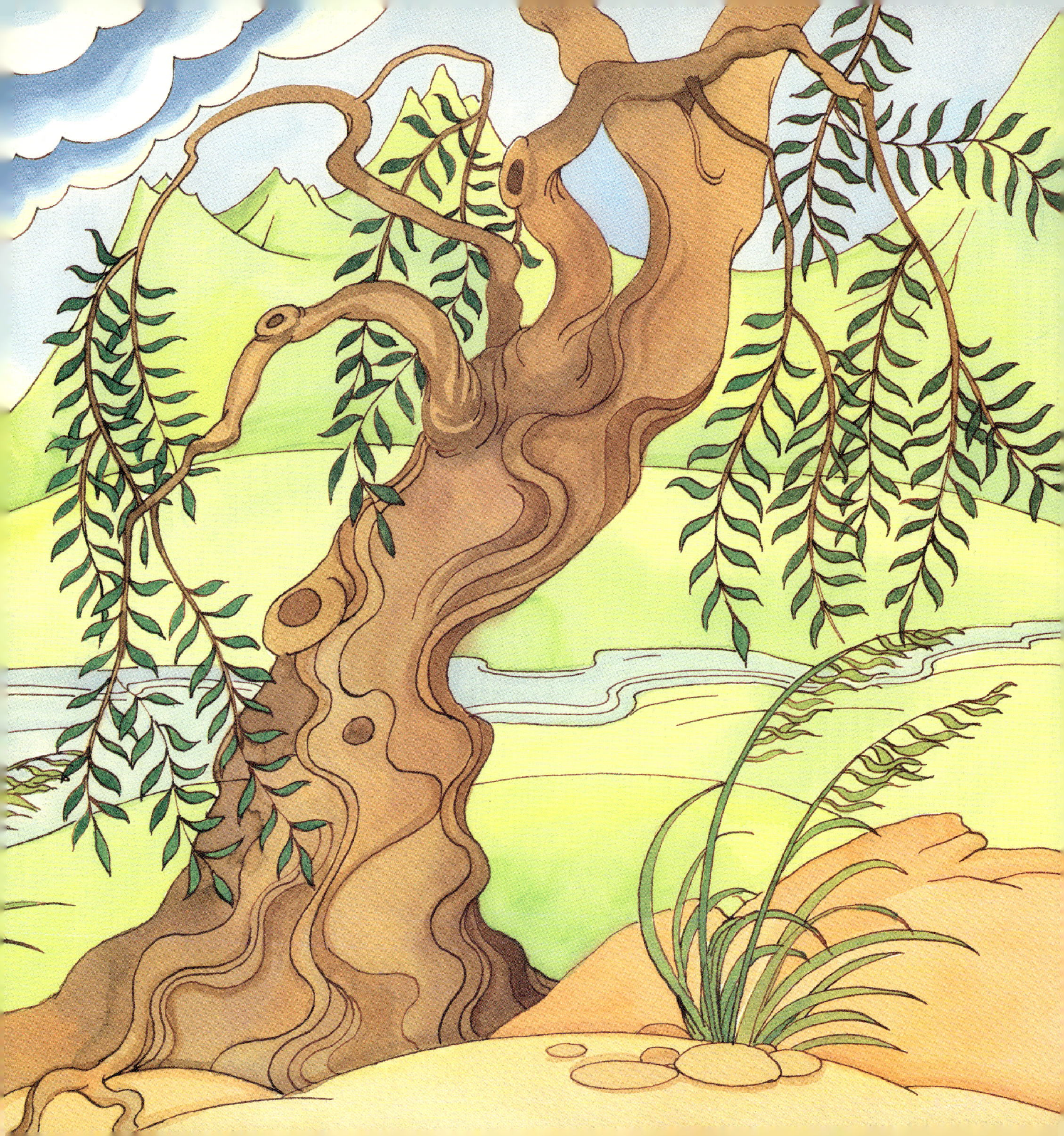